To:

_____

*A gift to prayerfully remind you of the
promises available to us all*

From:

_____

Prayers and Promises

Marie Jones
Margaret Anne Huffman

new seasons
™

a division of Publications International, Ltd.

Louis Weber, CEO
Publications International, Ltd.
7373 North Cicero Avenue
Lincolnwood, Illinois 60712

ISBN: 0-7853-5422-0

Contents

The Promise of God's Presence

And remember,
I am with you always, to the
end of the age.

Matthew 28:20

*L*ord, you are here,
Lord, you are there.
You are wherever we go.
Lord, you guide us,
Lord, you protect us.
You are wherever we go.
Lord, we need you,
Lord, we trust you,
You are wherever we go.
Lord, we love you,
Lord, we praise you,
You are wherever we go.

Chant of the Dinka tribe of the Southern Sudan

The guardian angels
of life sometimes fly
so high as to be out of sight,
but they are always looking
down on us.

Jean Paul Richter

It helps me, O God,
to look over my shoulder
and see times where you
were a ready companion.
I rest secure, knowing
that you are already
waiting to take my hand
into tomorrow.

When we shift
our focus beyond the physical,
we realize we exist amidst a
presence and power that
is transcendent.

*M*y trust is in you,
God of miracles and surprises,
for daily I feel your presence
in a dozen ways.

*W*hat a relief in this
throwaway world
of ever-changing values
to know that you,
O God, are the same yesterday,
today, and tomorrow.
Your trustworthiness and
desire for all your children
to have good things never varies.
You are as sure
as sunrise and sunset.

Although the rain
still falls, Creator God,
it takes such a little bit of
sun to create a rainbow,
your sign of promise
and presence.

humans and animals alike,
O Lord. How precious is your
steadfast love, O God!

Psalm 36:5–7

$\mathcal{L}$ike children with pail
and shovel trying
to empty the ocean
into a hole dug in the sand,
O God, we can't begin
to fathom the enormity
of the love with which
you long to fill us.

Lord, dismiss us with
thy blessing,
Hope, and comfort
from above;
Let us each,
thy peace possessing,
Triumph in redeeming love.

Robert Hawker

The steadfast love
of the Lord never
ceases, his mercies never
come to an end;
they are new
every morning; great
is your faithfulness.

Lamentations 3:22–23

*M*ercy is not something
we need beg of you, O God,
for your pleasure is to love us.
Mercy, grace, and love are
always available to us,
Lord, for you are always
available to us.

O Holy Creator,
who hath bound together
heaven and earth,
let me walk through your
kingdom comforted
and protected by the
warm rays of your love.
Let me be healed as I stand
basking in the divine
light of your presence,
where strength
and hope and joy are found.

Let me sit at rest
in the valley of your peace,
surrounded by the fortress of
your loving care.

The Promise
of Peace

Ah, what solace there is
in your promise of peace.
True help and real peace are
to be found from trusting
in your guidance
and inspiration.

Spirit, carry me
like a feather upon the current
to a place of serenity.

Let the waters flow over me
like cleansing balm.
Set me upon the dry place,
where life begins anew.
Spirit, carry me like a feather
back home again.

*Y*es, Father in heaven,
often have we found that
the world cannot give us peace,
O but make us feel that thou art
able to give us peace;
let us know the truth of thy
promise: that the whole world
may not be able to take
away thy peace.

Søren Kierkegaard

Peace I leave with you; my peace I give to you.

John 14:27

Lord,
bring me to the place
where peace flows like a river,
where soft green grasses
gently hold the weight of
my tired body,
where the light of a new
sunrise casts warmth.

The Promise of God's Bounty

Ask, and it will be given you;
search, and you will find; knock,
and the door will be opened for you.
For everyone who asks receives,
and everyone who searches finds,
and for everyone who knocks,
the door will be opened.

Matthew 7:7–8

For my part, I will sing of your
strength; I will celebrate
your love in the morning;
For you have become
my stronghold,
A refuge in the day of my trouble.
To you,
O my Strength will I sing;
For you,
O God are my stronghold and my
merciful God.

The Book of Common Prayer

*O*pen my eyes, so that I may
behold wondrous things.

Psalm 119:18

*M*ore things
are wrought by prayer
than this
world dreams of.

Alfred Lord Tennyson

O God,
giver of all good things,
our faith in you is like treasure
to be mined—it sustains,
it inspires, and it provides us with
unimagined contentment.

Have faith in God.
Truly I tell you,
if you say to this mountain,
"Be taken up and thrown
into the sea,"
and if you do not doubt
in your heart,
but believe that what
you say will come to pass,
it will be done for you.
So I tell you,
whatever you ask for

in prayer, believe that you
have received it, and it
will be yours.

Mark 11:22–24

The Promise of Life

Give us eyes with which to see,
noses with which to sniff,
ears with which to hear the faintest
sound along the paths you have
set for us, O God of Daily Joys.
Following you is a whole
experience—body, mind, and soul.

Holy Spirit,
the life that gives life.
You are the cause of
all movement;
You are the breath of
all creatures;
You are the salve that
purifies our souls;
You are the ointment that
heals our wounds;

You are the fire that
warms our hearts;
You are the light that
guides our feet.
Let all the world praise you.

Hildegard of Bingen

O Lord,
you are our Father;
we are the clay,
and you are our potter;
we are all the work of
your hand.

Isaiah 64:8

The Promise of Love

Your steadfast love,
O Lord, extends to the
heavens, your faithfulness
to the clouds.
Your righteousness is like
the mighty mountains,
your judgments are like
the great deep; you save

$\mathcal{O}$ heavenly Father,
protect and bless all things
that have breath;
guard them from all evil,
and let them sleep in peace.

Albert Schweitzer

We thank thee,
O Lord whose finger touched our dust,
O Lord who gave us breath.
We thank thee, Lord who gave us
sight and sense
to see the flower,
to hear the wind,
to feel the waters in our hand,
to sleep with the night and wake
with the sun,
to stand upon this earth,
to sing thy praise,
to hear thy voice.

*L*ord,
may I be wakeful at sunrise to
begin a new day for you,
cheerful at sunset for having done
my work for you;
thankful at moonrise
and under starshine for the beauty
of the universe.
And may I add what little may be
in me to your great world.

The Abbot of Greve

I am grateful, God of Hope,
for the gift of each new day,
each new season,
like the one unfolding around me
now in flower and birdsong,
in seedling and bud.
When they arrive as surely as
dawn follows night and
bloom follows bulb,
I am uplifted by the fulfillment
of your promise.

The Promise of Grace

Dear God, your love
embraces me like the warmth of the sun,
and I am filled with light.

Your hope enfolds me in arms so strong,
I lack for nothing.
Your grace fills me with the strength
I need to move through this day.
For these gifts you give me,
of eternal love, eternal peace,
and most of all, eternal friendship,
I thank you, God.

The grace of the living God
refreshes like cool,
clear water on a hot day,
giving our parched souls
the sustenance and
nourishment they need.

O most merciful Lord,
grant to me thy grace, that it may be
with me, and labour with me, and
persevere with me even to the end.
Grant that I may always desire and will
that which is to thee most acceptable,
and most dear. Let thy will be mine,
and my will ever follow thine,
and agree perfectly with it. Grant to me
above all things that can be desired,
to rest in thee, and in thee to have
my heart at peace.

Thomas à Kempis

Blessings, like miracles,
appear only when
we believe in them.
Faith gives us the eyes with
which to see, and to believe
what we see.

How grateful we are,
God of Knowledge, that you
created us so curious.
In your wisdom, it is the searcher
turning over every leaf who finds
four-leaf clovers;
the doubter who invents;
and the determined,
like a duckling pecking its way
from the shell, who emerges
strong enough to fly.

All I have seen teaches
me to trust the Creator for all
I have not seen.

Ralph Waldo Emerson

God's love and grace are
always available to us.
We have but to cast our eyes
heavenward to see that the
doors to God's kingdom are
always open.

Marie Jones is an ordained minister and a widely published writer of articles and essays. She is the creator/producer of Gigglebug Farms *Simply Storybook* Children's Videos. She is a contributing author to numerous books, including *Small Keepsake: Sister* and *Mother's Daily Prayer Book*.

Margaret Anne Huffman has been an award-winning journalist and former lifestyle editor of the *Shelby News*. She has written and contributed to many books, including *An Angel by Your Side*, *My Personal Daily Prayer Book*, and *Silver Linings: Friends*. Special acknowledgment and sympathy is extended to the family and friends of Margaret Anne Huffman, who passed away in November 2000.